THE NATURE KIDS GUIDE TO

DEER

DAVID ANDERSON

LP Media Inc. Publishing
Text copyright © 2026 by LP Media Inc.
All rights reserved.

For information address LP Media Inc. Publishing,
30012 Variolite St NW, Princeton MN 55371
www.lpmedia.org

Publication Data

Deer
The Nature Kid's Guide to Deer — First edition.

Summary: "Learn all about Deer, the Nature Kid Way"
— Provided by publisher.

ISBN: 979-8-89818-095-9

[1. Deer – Non-Fiction] I. Title.

Title: The Nature Kid's Guide to Deer

CONTENTS

FOREST FRIENDS

Rustle! A deer steps through the trees. Its big ears turn to listen.

Deer live on every continent except Antarctica and Australia. They make their homes in forests, meadows, and swamps. Some deer live high on mountains, while others prefer open grasslands.

Deer need plants to eat and water to drink. They also need safe places to rest and hide. Thick bushes and tall grass give them spots to stay safe from danger.

Forests give deer everything they need. Trees provide shade in summer. Fallen leaves make soft beds.

DEER EVERYWHERE

Snap! A deer walks across dry leaves. It sniffs the air.

Deer can live in many different habitats. They make their homes in forests, grasslands, and even swamps.

Some deer live in thick woods with tall trees. Others live in open meadows with soft grass.

Deer are very adaptable animals. They can find food and shelter almost anywhere. This helps them survive in hot deserts, snowy mountains, and everything in between.

Reindeer are the only deer species where both males and females grow antlers.

BIG
BUCKS

Thump! A large buck lands after a jump. It stands tall.

Deer come in many sizes. The smallest deer is called a pudu. It stands only 14 inches tall. That is shorter than a house cat!

The largest deer is the moose. A moose can weigh up to 1,800 pounds. It stands taller than a horse.

Most deer weigh between 100 and 300 pounds. Males are usually bigger than females.

Moose antlers can weigh 40 pounds and span 6 feet wide. They regrow yearly.

AMAZING ANTLERS

Deer antlers can grow up to half an inch every day! That's one of the fastest growing bones in the animal kingdom.

Crack! Two bucks push their antlers together to test their strength.

Male deer grow antlers, but females do not. These bony branches grow from the top of their heads. They are made of hard bone.

Antlers start growing in spring. Soft skin called **velvet** covers them. This skin brings blood to help the antlers grow fast. By fall, the velvet dries up and falls off.

Deer use their antlers to fight other males. They push and shove to show who is strongest.

Each year, deer shed their antlers and grow new ones!

SUPER
SENSES

Snort! A doe lifts her head. Her nose twitches fast.

Deer have amazing senses. Their large ears can turn in different directions. This helps them hear sounds from all around.

A deer's nose is very powerful. It can smell predators from far away.

Deer have eyes on the sides of their heads. They can see nearly all around without moving.

Deer can see in almost total darkness using special eye cells called rods. These cells are very sensitive to light and help deer spot movement at night when predators are hunting.

HIDDEN HELPERS

Whoosh! A deer's white tail flashes as it runs away.

Deer have special ways to stay safe. **Camouflage** helps hide deer from predators. Their brown fur blends in with trees and bushes.

Baby deer have spots on their fur. These spots look like sunlight on the forest floor. This helps baby deer hide in tall grass.

Adult deer raise their white tails when they sense danger. This warns other deer to run away.

Deer can rotate their ears in different directions to hear danger coming.

MUNCHING
MENU

Crunch! A buck bites into a leafy branch. It chews slowly.

Deer are **herbivores**. This means they only eat plants. They munch on grass, leaves, and twigs.

In spring and summer, deer find lots of food. They eat green plants, flowers, and berries. Some deer also like acorns and nuts.

Winter is harder. Then deer eat bark and dried leaves. They dig through snow to find food that is hidden underneath.

Deer can eat over 600 different kinds of plants, even poison ivy!

SPEAKING DEER

Snort! A deer stamps its foot on the ground.

Deer make many sounds. Does call to their fawns with soft bleats. Fawns answer with high squeaks. Bucks grunt during fall months. A loud snort means danger is near.

Deer use their feet to communicate. They stomp their front hooves on the ground. This warns other deer that danger is near. The thumping sound and motion grab attention fast.

Smell is important too. Deer have scent glands on their faces and legs. They rub these on trees and bushes. Other deer can smell these marks. This tells them who has been there.

20

Growl! A wolf watches a deer from behind some trees.

Many animals hunt deer. Wolves, coyotes, and mountain lions are common **predators**. Bears also catch deer when they can.

Deer must stay alert to detect nearby danger. Their eyes watch for movement. Their ears listen for sounds. Their noses smell for predators too.

Young fawns face the most danger of all. Even Eagles and bobcats will hunt small fawns. Mother deer try hard to protect their babies.

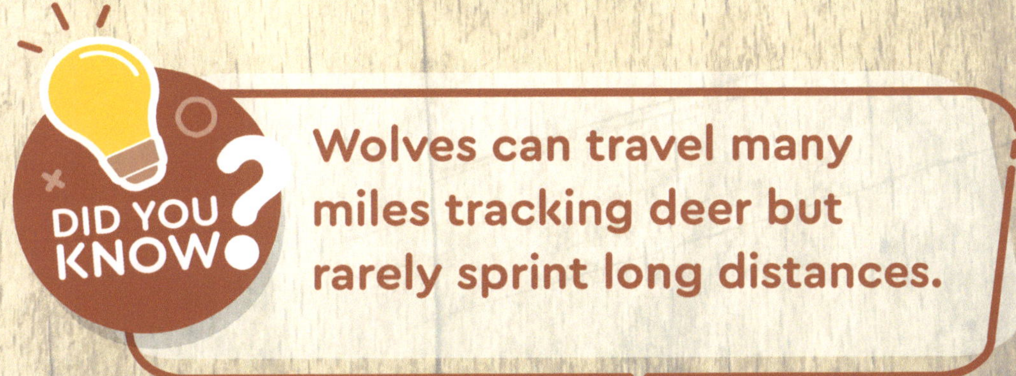

DASH AWAY

Swoosh! A deer races through tall grass. Its legs blur with speed.

Deer can sprint up to 30 miles per hour. This speed helps them escape predators like wolves and coyotes.

They leap over fences and logs with ease. One jump can reach 10 feet high! Their strong back legs give them this power.

Scared deer also run in zigzags. Quick turns confuse predators and help deer escape.

LEAP ALONG

Splash! A deer bounds across a stream, sending water flying into the air.

Deer are great jumpers. Their long legs push off the ground with force. They can leap over bushes and fallen trees.

Deer also swim well. They cross rivers and lakes to find food or escape danger.

In deep snow, deer walk in single file. They step in each other's tracks to save energy.

A deer can leap forward about 20 to 30 feet in one bound. That's nearly as long as a school bus!

UP AT DAWN

Chirp! Birds sing as a deer wakes up. It stretches and looks around.

Deer are most active at dawn and dusk. These times are called **crepuscular** hours. Low light helps deer hide from predators.

In the morning, deer search for food. They munch on plants while the air is cool. By midday, most deer rest in shady spots.

At dusk, deer become active again. They feed until darkness falls.

Deer have no upper front teeth! They use a tough pad on the roof of their mouth to tear plants instead.

HERD LIFE

Grunt! A group of deer grazes in a meadow together.

Female deer often live in groups called herds. A deer herd can have five to twenty animals. Does and their fawns stay close together.

Herds help deer stay safe. Many eyes watch for danger. If one deer spots trouble, all the others know.

Male deer usually live alone. They join herds during mating season.

Some deer herds follow the same doe leader for many years. Her experience helps keep the herd safe from danger!

BUCK BATTLE

Crack! Two bucks face each other. Their sharp antlers crash into each other.

Male deer fight to show strength. These battles happen in fall during mating season. Bucks lower their heads and charge at each other.

Their antlers crash together with loud sounds. The bucks push and shove. Each one tries to force the other back.

Most fights end quickly. The weaker buck walks away. Serious injuries are rare.

Male deer can lose about 10 to 20 percent of their body weight during the mating season.

FAWN SPOTS

Squeak! A tiny fawn lies in tall grass. Its spotted coat blends in.

Baby deer are called fawns. They are born with white spots on their backs. These spots look like sunlight on the forest floor.

The spots help fawns hide. Predators have trouble seeing them in the grass. Fawns stay very still when danger is near.

Most fawns lose their spots after a few months. Their coats turn solid brown like adult deer. By winter, the spots are completely gone.

A newborn fawn can stand up within twenty minutes of being born. It can walk within an hour.

DOE DUTY

Bleat! A doe nudges her fawn. She licks its soft fur clean.

Mother deer take care of their babies alone. Bucks do not help raise fawns.

A doe visits her fawn several times each day. She feeds it milk and cleans its fur. Between visits, the fawn hides alone in tall grass.

Does protect their young from danger. A mother may stomp at small predators or lead her fawn to safety.

Fawns stay with their mother for about one year.

DID YOU KNOW? A doe makes soft sounds to call her hidden fawn out of tall grass.

36
MULE DEER

A hiker spots a deer on a mountain trail. It's Mule deer.

Mule deer get their name from their large ears. Their ears are big and shaped like a mule's ears. White-tailed deer have much smaller ears.

Mule deer tails look different too. They are white with a black tip. White-tailed deer have wide brown tails with white undersides.

Mule deer also run in a unique way. They bounce with all four feet hitting the ground at once. This is called stotting. White-tailed deer run with a smooth gallop instead.

Mule deer can survive in the desert by getting water from the plants they eat, sometimes going days without drinking.

DEER DETECTIVE

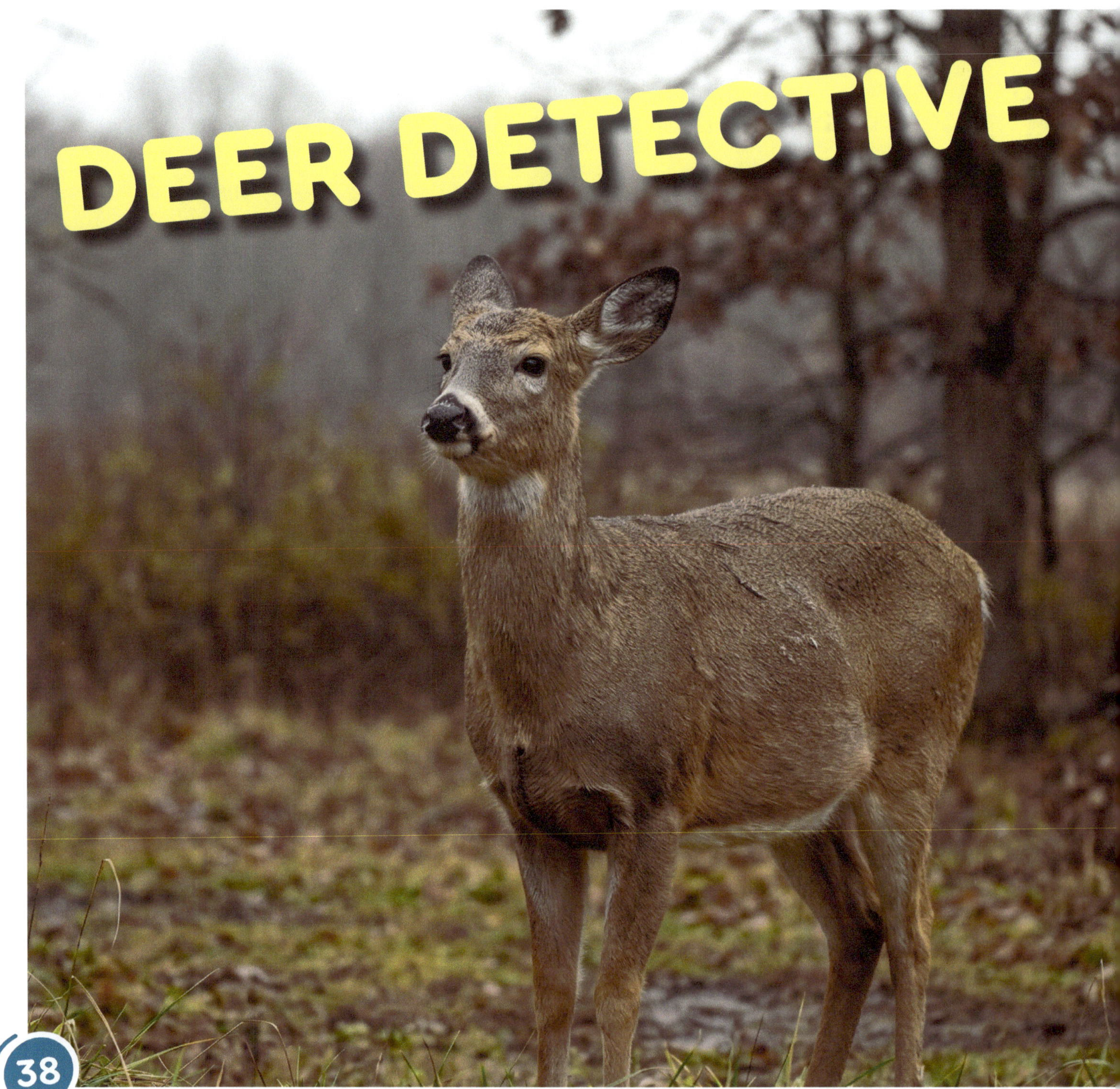

Rustle! A deer lifts its head. Its ears turn toward a sound.

You can be a deer detective! Look for clues that deer leave behind. Hoof prints in mud show where deer walked.

Deer rub their antlers on trees. This leaves marks on the bark. You might find tufts of fur on low branches.

The best time to spot deer is dawn or dusk. They come out to eat when light is dim. Stay quiet and still to watch them.

Deer droppings look like small, dark pellets. Finding them means deer visit that spot often.

GLOSSARY

herbivores
Animals that only eat plants, not meat.

camouflage
Colors or patterns that help an animal hide by blending in with what's around it.

predators
Animals that hunt and eat other animals.

crepuscular
Active during the early morning and evening when the sun is low.

velvet
Soft, fuzzy skin that covers growing antlers and brings them blood.

www.ingramcontent.com/pod-product-compliance
Lightning Source LLC
Chambersburg PA
CBHW041612110726
48005CB00002B/370